Praise for *A Movie*

In *A Movie*, Courtney Bush presents us with a screen upon which we can view her virtuosic intelligence, pathos and wit, heart and ear in action. The result, *A Movie*, helps us understand that movies really are actually everything. I mean, really, everything! Movies are the magical invocations to a changed and better life. They're also products of impromptu corporations' intent on capitalizing upon our innermost signatures of feeling. They're projected on the universe's biggest screens and they're on in the background while we're doing something, anything, else. But above all, movies are things that we make, in the basement, in the classroom, in the studio and the streets. Like poetry they are the things we do with our friends. I left the theater of *A Movie* with wet and salty cheeks—tears of celebration of what this book has taught us and tears of gratitude for giving me the urgent feeling that I must immediately deliver my life kinetically into poetry—the highest compliment I can give.

Brandon Brown, author of *The Four Seasons*

You surface from a Courtney Bush book the same way you leave a matinee screening: dazed, altered, shocked back into time. *A Movie* is a wise and utterly unguarded testament to the reward of making art—what of the world we mark, manipulate, and set apart to make the rest more bearable. "The bright life," Bush reminds us, "is what Dante called the life outside the Inferno, the life he left behind." It is the bright life to which she returns us.

Jameson Fitzpatrick, author of *Pricks In The Tapestry*

A Movie documents the determined acts of collective fantasy and work that it takes to make a film, to "make images move." If I were to adapt this book for the screen, her syntax would be the main character—played by, say, Kate Winslet—honoring the source material by hiding a dark secret behind its beauty and directness: Bush loves, too, the stubborn work that viewers do, with their naps, their interruptions, their plot summaries, their partial views, to make the images stop.

    Rainer Diana Hamilton, author of *God Was Right*

If poetry was written true without the affectations and writerly tropes, you'd get something crystalline and pure such as Courtney Bush's *A Movie*. I've never read a book like this really, though I've never met a poet, (or person) like Courtney Bush in general. Part film criticism, part diary-of-an-artist, *A Movie* chronicles the speaker's idea and then attempts to make a sexy vampire film. But it's also a book about making art, and thinking about making art, and if you do either you'll want to read this too.

    Ben Fama, author of *Deathwish*

A Movie

Courtney Bush

Lavender Ink
New Orleans
lavenderink.org

A Movie
Courtney Bush

Copyright © 2025 Courtney Bush and Lavender Ink.

All rights reserved. No part of this work may be reproduced in any form without the express written permission of the copyright holders.

Printed in the U.S.A.

Designer: Sean F. Munro
Cover: photographs by Courtney Bush, Jessa Ross, Will Carington & Jake Goicoechea

Publisher's Cataloging-in-Publication Data
Names: Bush, Courtney.
Title: A movie / Courtney Bush.
Description: New Orleans, LA : Lavender Ink, 2025. | Summary: A poem written in sentences revolving around the phrase "a movie," written by a filmmaker and including the narrative of writing, directing, and acting in a short vampire movie.
Identifiers: LCCN 2024950059 | ISBN 9781956921397 (pbk.)
Subjects: LCSH: American poetry – 21st century. | Motion picture authorship – Poetry. | COVID-19 (Disease) – Poetry. | BISAC: POETRY / American / General. | POETRY / Subjects & Themes / General. | POETRY / Women Authors.
Classification: LCC PS3602.U8357 M68 2025 | DDC 811.6–dc23
LC record available at https://lccn.loc.gov/2024950059

Lavender Ink
lavenderink.org

this one's for Michael Douglas

A Movie

As I waited in the dark theater for the Secret Life of Pets 2 to begin, my arm brushed against the soft forearm of the woman beside me.

The 7th floor theater at Regal Court Street was packed on the hottest day of Brooklyn summer.

My edible kicked in during the first trailer.

I traced a heart in the sweat on my large Diet Coke.

I watched a famous actor stutter onscreen in 19th century New York, trying to make his way in the New World, which would be hard enough without the speech impediment.

I watched a supercut of the man as he gained confidence in public speaking at the hand of a mentor.

This was a popular subgenre of movie at the time.

A man in the past tries to lose his stutter.

It was simply Edward Norton's turn.

Old fashioned gas lamps, Coney Island in CGI.

The score built in meaning, more gold blended into the color grade with each passing frame.

Can you believe it used to look like this? it seemed to ask.

No, because it didn't.

A woman with a tiny waist and billowing skirt, like the skirts through a window in a Frank O'Hara poem, waited for Edward Norton on the Brooklyn Bridge.
We are told the movie will be out in time for Thanksgiving.

The woman beside me, swallowed for a moment in the darkness between trailers, said with calm disgust:

They just wanted to make a movie.

When I was a child in South Mississippi, it didn't occur to me that a movie was made by an actual human being.

We were only on the distribution pathways of huge films that could make money in a megaplex-style movie theater.

First, we went to Courthouse Cinema, a low, sturdy building from the 80s with star-patterned carpet, kept cool even in the extreme summer heat.

It was located in a complex next to a pizza restaurant called Brooklyn's, a Subway, and a liquor store.

The lights in the parking lot were square shaped, and they were always on when the movie was over.

Courthouse Cinema had two arcade games in one corner.

My mom would often drop off my little sister and me to see whatever movie was playing on a Saturday.

I folded the dollar bills into my pocket which we would use for popcorn or a drink or a pickle from a giant jar in which a teenager would fish with tongs.

We used whatever money we had left to play the games after the movie while we waited for the black Volvo to appear and pick us up under the square-shaped lights of the parking lot.

A new, better movie theater was built in the early 2000s at a brand-new shopping center only fifteen minutes further away than Courthouse.

Cinemark had reclining stadium seats, flavored powders you could put on your popcorn, and a restaurant with ice cream.

I'm still annoyed at my child self for loving Cinemark more than Courthouse, for abandoning Courthouse to the fate of slowly dying places.

I'm sure there were independent cinemas somewhere in Mississippi, maybe in Oxford or Starkville near the universities, but there wasn't anything like that near us.

At Cinemark we saw This Is 40, Knocked Up, Pineapple Express.

Some of them several times.

I guess I mostly remember the Judd Apatow movies there.

Action movies, superhero movies, movies about outer space.

I hated all of those, except for Iron Man.

When I was a teenager, I gravitated back to Courthouse, which was steadily becoming more and more dilapidated.

This is what drew me back.

I loved the disgusting upholstery, the broken chairs.

I was at Courthouse Cinema when I realized that people make movies, and at the same time, when I realized I hadn't known that before.

I remember the exact moment.

I was sitting in the back row with Katelyn Glenn, a girl from school who I smoked weed with sometimes.

We were watching Inglourious Bastards by Quentin Tarantino, of all movies, of all directors.

When the female lead smears lipstick on her cheeks like warpaint while David Bowie sings about fighting fire with gasoline, I saw it.

Somebody had made this decision.

Only a person could've made this decision.

I understood, in that moment, a movie is a series of human decisions.

I started to cry.

Later, I came to the learn that the decisions were not always made by a person.

That sometimes tradition made the decisions.

Most often, the market made the decisions.

Money made the decisions.

Politics and convention and racism and sexism made the decisions.

Sometimes tradition and the market and politics and money made cool decisions, too, I guess.

Sometimes innovation happened even then.

Still, I'm glad my younger self had that moment in the theater next to Katelyn Glenn, believing that every movie was a series of decisions a human being had made, which still feels true in some way even though of course it's not.

I always want to make a movie, but I try to do less these days.

These days after a neurological event reminded me to change the station, warm up the input socket and don't worry so much.

These days I am soothed by the contents of my refrigerator, the soup I made in the pressure cooker with very few ingredients.

The barley salad a friend's mother used to make once a week in Geneva.

The almond butter from the cheap place that will close and force me to find another cheap place, the next one even further away.

But I love to walk and even more to walk while carrying something heavy.

I wear something thick to protect my shoulder from the grinding of the bag strap.

The things I wear deteriorate slowly, over time, and will be thrown out.

I eat handfuls of spinach straight from the bag, standing over the sink.

But still, in the back of all that, I know I want to make a movie.

That I'll always want to make another movie.

Just when I was trying to do less, after all the film festivals Jake, Will and I were supposed to go to with our last movie were cancelled because of the pandemic, and after we had gotten over the fact that all the film festivals were cancelled, we got an email from a festival in Toronto that said we were invited to pitch a short film in a competition to win some money for the production of that film.

The competition would, of course, be virtual.

We could win 5000 Canadian dollars.

With 5000 Canadian dollars, we could at least make part of a movie.

I told them no, I don't want to do it.

They said but, but, do you really not?

Of course I did, but what movie would we pitch? We don't have a movie.

Your vampire movie, they said.

But we haven't written the vampire movie, I said.

I can't do it, I said, then turned my phone over, face down on the rug.

I started watching a movie in my living room.

When the pandemic started, I finally bought a TV, which made my life better and worse, like everything new does.

The movie I watched was called Food, Gas, Lodging by Allison Anders.

Unfortunately for me, who was trying very hard not to want to, it was one of those movies that made me want to make a movie.

While the end credits rolled, while a song called Love with wildly swinging vocals played over the names of the unbelievable amount of people it takes to make a movie, even a tiny movie, I took to my phone to tell them I would write the movie as long as I didn't have to write the pitch.

I decided I could write a movie, but to then write about the movie, to explain what it was, why it might have value?

That I could not do.

I took a stack of multi-colored index cards out of the top drawer of the pink cabinet and sat down on the wood floor, where I like to write in the beginning, where I like to move the cards around.

The skylight warmed the apartment, but did not make it unbearably hot like in summer.

It was spring.

I opened the window.

I enjoyed the warmth of the blonde wood floor and laid down on it for breaks.

And, for the record, three days later, once I'd written the script, I did have to write the pitch.

But first, on the sun-warmed floor, I had to recall the conversations, the snippets of feeling which were the beginning of the vampire movie, the movie that had been gestating for over a year, the movie I had just committed to writing in the next 36 hours.

When the germ of the vampire movie had entered my mind, I had been walking with Rozz around the loop of Prospect Park, back when there were fewer swans in the pond than there are now.

We talked about the way certain people are like vampires, the way they lean in and absorb your stories, your personality traits, your life.

We had recently been fucked with by a woman like that who tried to take away our best friend.

She was a party girl, coked out and fun all the time.

She never slept.

She told me things about my best friend Jake as if she were introducing me to him.

She told me what kind of peanut butter he likes, which I of course already knew.

She posted photos of him all over social media.

Then, of course, she tried to scam her way into living in one friend's apartment, getting money from another friend, and made up a ton of lies about her job which it turns out she never really had.

Some people were traumatized, but I knew all along there was something about the girl.

I was wary of her from the start, the way one character in every horror movie is wary of the evil party from the beginning, but the significance of her wariness is usually covered up by her personality.

She's just a paranoid crazy girl, they say.

In two days, on the floor, I wrote a story about a paranoid crazy girl who becomes a vampire slayer.

I wrote about a party girl vampire who wants to be a human, who wants stories, memories, personality, a life.

I had the characters quote the scene from Twilight.

I know what you are.

Say it.

Which we eventually cut from the script.

I sent the draft to Jake and Will.

This is the first and easiest part of making a movie.

In this way it is deceptive.

The deception is important, because if you didn't deceive yourself into thinking you could do all the things required to make your movie, you would never start making your movie.

As always, the more of the movie I wrote, the longer I thought about it, the more I realized just how much I did want to make the movie.

How I had wanted to make this movie for years.

How making a twenty minute movie about a vampire, in some ways, was all I had ever wanted to do.

How I was afraid if I did get the opportunity to do it, I wouldn't be able to make the vampire movie in my mind, the one I had been dreaming of, unbeknownst to me, since I was born.

I was afraid it wouldn't be good enough.

I was afraid of failing at something only I could possibly succeed at.

But I told myself that it was okay, I didn't need to worry, because we probably wouldn't win the Canadian money anyway.

When I got to college at NYU and met students who knew the names of directors, I used to joke that the only movie I had ever seen was the House Bunny.

The House Bunny is actually an amazing movie, but that was my joke.

My first friend in college was in the Cinema Studies program.

I was afraid of how much knowledge Andy had.

I did whatever he said. I watched whatever movie he mentioned. I ordered the DVDs from Netflix like a religious penance and watched them on my laptop on the bunk in my dorm.

I went to every screening he asked me to go to.

I watched my first Woody Allen movie, then my second, third, eighth, tenth, and so on.

Love and Death was my favorite.

I watched Breathless, Pierrot Le Fou.

I watched Apocalypse Now and Dr. Strangelove and everything involving Peter Sellars.

I was embarrassed when I didn't know Peter Sellers was dead in a room full of people who did.

I saw an 8-hour biopic of Che Guevara that year.

We went to a movie palace from 1929 out in Jersey City to see Chinatown.

She's my daughter, she's my sister, she's my daughter and my sister.

Forget it, Jake. It's Chinatown.

We saw the original Dracula with a live organist.

I went with him to Film Forum to see a Charlie Chaplin double feature, where I was deeply disturbed by the way people laughed at the humor.

They laughed out loud, with a grating pride in the fact that they were laughing. Here, now, at this.

This type of humor isn't to be laughed at now. It makes absolutely no sense. We have changed, I thought. Everything has changed.

This is fake, I thought. Why would they do this, I thought.

I heard once that if you are making a movie, and you want it to be an automatic success, you just have to get the audience to laugh thirteen times.

If you make someone laugh thirteen times, they will love the movie.

Sometimes, when I watch a movie, I try to count how many times I laugh.

I always lose count but I imagine it's usually zero, even when I love it.

My new boyfriend Kyle texts me from work.

I'd rather be watching Zombieland.

I'd rather be watching Zombieland 2.

The other day, taking care of Milo and Augie, I read to them from a book of stories based on a movie.

We read about Princess Anna and Princess Elsa.

I hate that movie.

Then we went into the treehouse in the yard of the big house outside the city where the children go on the weekends.

While they got in a little fight I read the notes scribbled and carved into the wooden planks left by people before, many of them writing the name of the boy who must've lived in this house.

Owen. Brie loves Owen. Hi Owen! Best summer Ever 1998.

Since many of the inscriptions were dated I followed a thread of Owen's life.

Male friends' names repeated over the years, but the girls' names changed.

I read "2022 last treehouse box sesh" and realized that the boy, Owen, now surely an adult, had gotten to say goodbye to this treehouse on his terms, with the same friends who had been here.

This made me first jealous.

Then sad, then I was suddenly horrified by a permanence like that.

What it might do to a person.

The privilege of being able to say goodbye in the exact way you want to is not something I think we are supposed to experience.

Then Augie fell from a swing and busted his lip.

Blood poured over his brand-new teeth.

I don't feel adequate to language that is too exciting, too different from the way we speak it when we just want the listener to understand.

That night we watched a movie.

It was the older child's turn to choose.

Milo wanted to watch Beetlejuice.

I said, no, it's too scary for you.

He cried and begged, so I said take it easy, fine, we'll watch it.

He couldn't sleep that night.

The following day he said Courtney next time the grown-ups tell me a movie is too scary and I say I want to watch it, don't let me watch it, okay?

He told me that during the night, he was so tired of being scared that he stood in the middle of his room and said Beetlejuice, Beetlejuice, Beetlejuice, to see if he was real.

Beetlejuice did not come to Milo's room, so he must not be real.

Still, Milo was terrified.

I told him I was proud of him for being so brave.

Of course, we won the Canadian money.

And this is how.

In a Zoom chatroom, we met the other filmmakers who would be pitching their projects to a group of judges comprised of LGBTQIA filmmakers and writers and one drag queen from Rupaul's Drag Race.

One guy, who was Zooming in from Greece, was literally smoking a cigarette while he pitched his film, which was totally incoherent and would not win.

I realized in this Zoom meeting, as I have realized in so many spaces in my life, that most people really don't know how to make baseline sense.

We had that advantage.

There are so many things that Jake and Will and I don't know how to do, but we do know how to make sense.

We described in clear terms that we wanted to make a movie with female vampires, a gay male oracle figure, and no straight men.

We wanted to gesture more to the some of the early films of the vampire genre and less to the modern iterations.

How would we do that, specifically? A writer from some magazine asked. What films, exactly, do you want to gesture to?

When someone asks me a question, it's hard for me to not undertake it as a challenge.

I am competitive by nature.

I gave a beautiful answer about how we were inspired by the movie Vampyr, which was made on the cusp of talkies, so that it featured lines of dialogue but maintained the silent film technique of title cards for exposition.

We want to go in the opposite direction of the indie movie convention where the viewer drops into an ongoing scene and has to figure out for himself what's happening.

In a vampire movie from 1929, before you see a frame of movement, you read a card that explains to you a professor who studies infectious disease has traveled to a small town in Romania to investigate the local superstition of an immortal creature who feeds on the blood of the living.

We want to do something like that.

This answer pleased the judges, possibly because we were the only group of filmmakers to pitch a film instead of some tangle of ideas.

In any case, it pleased them enough to give us 5000 Canadian dollars over Zoom.

Jake, Will, and I met up outside, bought a bottle of champagne and walked toward Fort Greene Park.

Jake let me wear his blue sunglasses.

On the way, we passed a window that was selling frozen drinks to go.

We bought strawberry margaritas in paper cups.

We sat in the grass, got completely shitfaced, smoked cigarettes, and realized we were actually going to be able to make a movie.

And "to be able to" is both true and also a nice framing of the fact that now we had to.

Lying on the blanket, we started working on the movie by talking about who would be in it.

Who did we know that could play the vampire?

Someone beautiful, someone we wish we could be, someone who seduces without trying, but someone who can also act in a way that doesn't make us want to peel our eyelids off, because most actors do.

We thought of our friend Michelle.

She would do it? Right? She loves us, right? We have a real connection?

We looked up at the lace of the leaves.

I wrote the oracle thinking of Payton, so it will have to be Payton, I said.

Will and Jake nodded.

And you, Jake said, obviously.

Me, I said, obviously, slamming my fist into the thick grass.

I would play the paranoid crazy girl who was named after Van Helsing.

Then we won't have to pay an actor, they said.

And because that character is you, they added.

I love the trope and the cue.

The slut, the fugue.

Oh God I love when the bell finally rings.

When Romy says we don't give a flying fuck what you think.

I love to love, but my baby just loves to dance.

I love when he sings I've got the blues, the reds and the pinks.

One thing's for sure, love stinks.

I love the torn shirt, the corn syrup, the knives.

I love the leaves blowing across the street in Haddonfield.

The rotary phone ringing at night.

I love the complicated relationship between brothers in the Mafia.

New Years in Cuba, you have broken my heart.

I love that green cake.

I've never seen a cake that color in real life.

I love the grindhouse pause for effect.

I love the PG-13 single-use fuck.

I love the murderer in the black cloak and I love his partner.

Love his accent.

His bloody teeth.

I love Sydney Prescott.

I love what is your favorite scary movie?

The way movies don't kill people, people kill people.

The pan, the zoom, the score coming in.

The pop song playing in the K-Mart.

The dancing boy, the tattooed girl.

The radio on his shoulder.

The hacker with the silver boots, the screen name, Winona.

I love the serial killer you never find.

I love the obsessive nerd, the hottest girl you've ever seen in your fucking life.

This is how I win. Remember that?

I love the Cellino and Barnes commercial playing on the TV in the background of Good Time.

I love when Robert Pattinson says I am better than you.

I love Bella. I love Edward. I am not Team Jacob.

I love when he sings this thing they call love is gonna make you cry/ I hate you.
The choreography, the stunt, the hidden cut, and the poorly hidden cut.

The director who is too afraid to leave the Netherlands.

I smile and I smile and I smile.

The grape jelly, the sound design, assigned seats in Norway.

The director who wears his own merch.

The director with the hair.

The one everybody loves.

The woman of the year who will be torn down, forgotten by the next awards season.

The nipples on the red carpet.

I love the director who died, the one who died the year before that.

The living one who is a poet, the dead one who was.

I love the original Blondie song for the soundtrack.

I love Hitchcock and the Hitchcock rip-offs.

The title, the extra, grip and key grip, whatever they do.

I love every detail, the unwatchable, the vague and meandering.

I love the insects in Tokyo, the homage within the homage.

I love the baseball movie.

I love the dirtied frame.

I love the 70s horror nonsensical breast reveal.

I love the Canadians.

I love the director who says I don't like to work.

I love the most disgusting person in the world.

The chicken fight and real fire.

The explosions in Road House.

The jump cut, eye contact, confessional.

The heiress, the orphan, the scamp.

When the two greatest actors of our lifetime sit across from each other in the restaurant.

I love the stupid girls who win.

I love the relentless cunt.

The conspiracy, the choking, the spell, the ditch in the dark just when you need it.

I love the death rattle, the thousand-foot drop, the yellow brick, the road.

Oh my god, the wish, the panic, the sweeping music, the dance in the gym.

I love the golden hair, the pyramid, the vengeance in her eyes.

I love the battle, every battle.

I love the most brilliant comedic performance Kirsten Dunst has ever given.

The first movie I ever loved was called All Dogs Go To Heaven.

The first movie my father ever loved was Mary Poppins.

The first movie my mother ever loved, to my knowledge, was The Rocky Horror Picture Show, but I assume there were earlier ones from her childhood.

I think of it as the first she ever loved because it was the first one she showed me framed as that particular kind of gift: a movie someone you love loves.

I was very young when I watched it.

I didn't know what sex was.

I never thought about gender.

I only knew I loved the way Tim Curry looked, the way he danced, the way he sneered and tapped the thick white and rhine-stoned heel of the kind of shoe I had never seen before.

A shoe I instantly loved.

Watching that movie made me feel like there were kinds of life possible beyond the ones I was aware of.

From my mother I also learned a new way of watching movies that I have come to call the kaleidoscopic method.

As an adult, the way I most often spend time with my mother, when I visit her quiet little house on a block of Biloxi, Mississippi that has been otherwise abandoned since Hurricane Katrina, is by watching movies together in her bed from morning to night.

Sometimes I nestle my head under her arm and rest my head against her breast while we watch.

Often, she sleeps and I am the only one watching.

Because she falls asleep so easily, and because she truly does want to watch the movie, when she wakes up, she decides whether she wants to just keep watching from wherever it is or if she wants to rewind the movie so she can piece it together.

It often goes like this.

Start a movie. Watch for a while. Fall asleep for a while. Watch some more. After a while go back to the beginning because though you've tried, you can't figure out what's going on with this one character. Did someone die? You start the movie over, but after a while, this time after having seen a bit more of the movie from the beginning, you fall asleep, and sleep for much longer. This time you wake up as the movie is resolving and the characters are on their way to finding peace, perhaps. Still feeling like you haven't really seen the movie, because, though it's now noon and you started this viewing just after breakfast, and though you've seen a lot of the movie, in a strange order, you really haven't quite seen it yet. This time, you start in the middle. You see parts of the movie you have never seen before. Inevitably, you fall asleep. You wake up later, you ask your daughter some questions and understand for a while, but something happens. You need clarity. You rewind it a bit. Watch a bit. This could go on forever, if you wanted, which is one of the many beauties of kaleidoscopic movie watching.

This winter, we watched Misery starring Kathy Bates and James Caan in this fashion.

While we watched, I tried to keep track of my mother's experience of the film.

For her, James Caan's injuries came and went.

The car wreck that incited the plot had happened, and then had not yet happened.

He finished the novel, smoked his cigarette and had his champagne.

Shortly thereafter, he had not yet begun writing.

After his ankles were hobbled by the woman who held him hostage, he met the woman, his ankles intact and healthy.

The woman was alive. She was dead. She was alive.

My mom said, I thought she died?

She did, but later, I replied.

She nodded and kept watching.

She did die, but later.

In this way, my mother experiences narrative time in new and interesting ways.

I'm honored you think I'm a hot vampire, our friend Michelle said, when she accepted the role.

We do, we admitted. We think you're beautiful and we know you're funny.

Michelle directs her own movies, brilliant movies that made us laugh.

She teaches movement. Every movement she makes is expressive, in life and in art.

I'm essentially a clown, she said, explaining the communicative power of her gestures. I can't help it.

We met with our producers Rozz and Anne-Louise on Zoom because Anne-Louise lives in Paris.

You should try to get someone famous, they said, without explaining how one might do that.

We set a date to start production.

This was during the pandemic, and one day, nothing happened, but we realized we weren't going to be able to do it.

We just didn't have the energy.

We had lost our confidence.

Something had happened.

We said let's wait a year.

The Canadian money will still be there.

A year later, a year in which nothing good happened and nobody could make movies, we decided to try again.

We needed an actor to play the gullible friend of the paranoid crazy girl.

Michelle recommended her friend Patrick who she had been friends with since undergraduate acting school.

I recognized his image when I Googled him.

He had just been nominated for a Pulitzer Prize in theater.

He came to Will's house to meet us.

Before he arrived, we arranged croissants and grapes on Will's nicest plates, the ones with gold flowers.

Trying to make him laugh, I told the story of when I had a colonic in a woman's apartment on the Upper West Side.

How her husband was in the next room, watching TV.

The apartment smelled like garlic.

Rozz and I had planned to get colonics together, based on her idea, which she got from the Kardashians' Instagram and their liver cleanse, where they posted pictures of these green stone-like things in the bottom of their toilet which they had apparently cleared from their liver.

After I'd told Rozz about my colonic experience, she opted out, even though I only did it because she wanted to.

Patrick laughed at my story and accepted the role but the day before he was supposed to be on set, he tested positive for asymptomatic Covid.

I secretly believed he didn't have Covid at all and it was the colonic story.

At the moment, I didn't have time to worry about it, because we needed a new actor that night.

Jake stepped in, and did a perfect job.

Another secret belief of mine is that almost anyone, as long as they are not an actor, is a better actor than an actor.

Unless they need to cry.

If you need someone to cry, you have to get an actor.

I woke up alone in the apartment desperate to watch a movie and scrolled through Criterion Channel.

I ended up with Gentlemen Prefer Blondes, because I just watched a Netflix documentary about Marilyn Monroe and how her complicated relationship with the Kennedys should factor into the way we think of her death.

I told Andy I watched that movie and he groaned, saying that Netflix always does that.

They release a documentary about someone just before they're about to release a movie about them.

Anna de Armas is going to play Marilyn Monroe, he said.

I wouldn't mind seeing that, but for now I am watching Jane Russell lip-synch her ass off in a room full of half-naked men.

And Marilyn herself wearing the ugliest purple outfit I've ever seen.

Now they are poisoning a man, while I check my email.

Another day I woke up alone and put on I Was A Teenage Zombie (1987).

During the first few frames, I realized it was shot at Brooklyn College, where I went to grad school.

There were the stairs where I used to talk on the phone as comfortably as if I were in my bedroom.

I paused the movie after the drug dealer character says, I remember the 60s.

It's the same now, except nobody cares anymore.

I played a Duran Duran record backwards last night. Do you know what happened?

What? the three college boys ask. What happened?

Absolutely nothing, the drug dealer says with deep sorrow.

I want to make a movie about an occult baseball coach.

Speaking Latin in the dugout to a writhing snake.

His players say in their Southern and Midwestern accents that they have no idea how he got the job, but he's a pretty great coach.

I want to make an Odyssey movie that is mostly men saying goodbye to their wives.

I asked a friend I ran into at a poetry reading how he was doing.

He said I'm living the dream.

I said that that was great to hear and asked him what the dream he was living was like.

He just told me what movies he had been watching.

Bergman Island.

Irma Vep.

I told my friend Shy I wanted to make a poem with magical properties, like certain poems we had been sending each other by Ariana Reines.

Shy said I don't think you could write a poem like that, but I think you could write a poem like a movie.

I started trying to write a poem like a movie.

I called it A Movie.

I wrote it in couplets.

It was long and made of memories and stories and moved fast between still images.

The only way I could think to write a poem like a movie was to engage moving images.

To try to somehow make images move, to increase the speed.

I looked at my long poem and it was nothing like a movie.

It was just like a poem, and a bad one, because I was trying and failing to make it be a movie.

At the end of my divorce, I dreamed a scene from an original movie.

It was the late 90s, I could tell from the clothing and the actors and the quality of light.

A large family makes their way out of a hospital room.

Meryl Streep, Stanley Tucci, Natasha Lyonne, Winona Ryder and the actress who plays Constanza in the Godfather.

Meryl Streep leaves the hospital room first, looking somber.

Stanley Tucci is next, smiling as if he'd said something funny, something wry, as he so often does.

Young Natasha Lyonne follows him with a wide smile of her own, briefly looking directly at the camera.

An even younger Winona Ryder comes out just after Natasha and gently pushes past her to reach Stanley Tucci, her brother in the movie, I think.

What she says to him in an absolutely perfect Winona intonation is this:

Aunt Mamie took the soda I just bought because she wanted a little sip, but then she gave it to Aunt Dot because she saw the soda and wanted a little sip too, but Dot drank half of it, and after that, she gave it to Aunt Katie...who drank the rest.

Stanley Tucci laughs sympathetically.

I knew somehow it was the first scene, then woke up.

I once made a movie with my friends in a house near the beach.

We had never before made a movie.

I left my horrible boyfriend in the city and for four days underwent the insanely stressful process of making a movie.

We were young.

We acted in the movie ourselves, because we didn't know where to find actors.

We drank real wine in the movie, so everyone got drunk.

We didn't know you're supposed to use fake wine.

We learned you can make a movie about night time during the day.

We covered all the windows of a friend of a friend's beach house with a thick black plastic called Visqueen and it became night inside.

We learned you can even make a movie about night time during the day while you're pretty drunk.

We were drinking real wine and lit the rug on fire when we didn't notice a fallen light.

The wine teeth we needed for the movie were our real teeth stained with real wine.

We didn't know about fake wine teeth.

We made a movie about something that really happened, and it hurt someone's feelings, which I did not anticipate.

I showed that red-wine-stained beach movie to a famous poet, who told me it's a shame I was overacting in the last scene and a shame that everyone was white.

Well one of the actors was Mexican but I didn't argue.

But he introduced me later that same day to a colleague at Brooklyn College as Courtney, who made a great movie.

He said my movie reminded him of certain Dogme 95 films, but I didn't know what that was, so when I got home I looked it up.

The Dogme 95 filmmakers, like me, wanted to make a movie.

They wanted to take away a lot of the things that had been put in place for making a movie, things that shouldn't be necessary if you are making a movie in the right spirit.

Additional lights, non-diegetic music and sound.

Such artifice had no place in a movie, they thought.

A movie like this is an act of the spirit, I think.

It can be an act of purity.

And all things must be stripped away from the spirit, if you want to make a movie of a very specific kind of purity.

One night, Will and I crossed Houston in the middle of the block, leaving Film Forum in the middle of winter.

We were leaving an evening showing of Drive My Car by Ryusuke Hamaguchi.

We hadn't yet broken the after-movie silence.

My mind was at work, I had learned something, I was taking something away.

I liked it, Will said.

I liked it, too.

What I liked was that it felt built, constructed from a very complicated blueprint which, once underway, could not be altered at any point or the entire structure would fall apart.

This blueprint was so confidently constructed it contained, but was also scaffolded by, several other works of art, some from the real world and some from within the world of the film.

A Chekhov play. The plots of fictional TV scripts.

To make a movie like that, there must be a moment, like crossing a street, where you say I am leaving that time behind, the time when questions can be asked, the time for tinkering and worrying and self-criticizing and editing, the time for healthy dissociation from the project, for the I'm not really doing anything, for the I don't really care about this.

But once you cross that street, you have to fully accept that you are going forward, that you will build the house, you will follow the blueprint.

That the plan you've made is sound. That your complicated building will stand up.

That your life depends on it. That it can, because you believe in its soundness.

It has to be that pure, I said. It has to be complete devotion. A kind of delusion.

That's the only way it will work, I said.

Will understood completely.

I said, I'm doing that now. With the vampire movie, okay? I won't do the thing I always do.

I won't leave my body while we're on set, float away somewhere safer.

I won't tell myself, secretly, this isn't what I do.

I'm a writer. This is just something else.

You do that? he asked.

I do that, I said. But not anymore.

I won't turn away from you, from Jake, from the project.

I will hold it and carry it until it's done, no matter what it takes.

We walked side by side and he said, yeah, but it doesn't have to be that serious. You have to, like, live.

No, I thought. I'm going to be that serious. I want to look at my film and see total devotion or I want to see nothing, I thought.

Sorry, I added. I'm getting carried away.

All I mean is that I liked it, I said. But I think I like his other movie more. Happy Hour, the 5-hour one on Criterion.

About the women?

And the conceptual artist?

And the short story writer?

And the baths at Arima?

Have you seen it?

One of my favorite books is about making a movie.

Werner Herzog wanted to make a movie about building an opera house in the rainforest, in an impossible place, but to do this he soon realized he was actually going to have to build the impossible opera house in the impossible rainforest.

In the book he remembers, "A fairly young, intelligent looking man with long hair asked me whether filming or being filmed could do harm, whether it could destroy a person.

In my heart the answer was yes, but I said no."

On the set of that movie, several indigenous people died trying to do the work Herzog had hired them to do.

But I don't know whether or not they were the ones in his heart when he answered the question.

When I want to watch a movie, I almost always want to watch a horror movie and I wonder if it is because I have experienced so few real horrors directly.

I lived a childhood fairly devoid of demons.

I don't even fear possession.

I think it could be interesting to be possessed, and who's to say I'm not already.

Having the devil's baby, a cursed videotape, a girl in the well, flowers colored black, whatever.

Nothing threatened me in the dark but the dark itself.

And a movie comes out of the dark, being made of light.

My mother, who also likes horror movies, sometimes reaches a limit that I think has to do with the real horrors she has actually experienced.

Once, watching a movie with a lot of gun fighting, she looked at me and said I'm so tired of this shit.

I can't look at any more of this shit today.

I thought about how her brother was killed by two gunshots, no one quite knows by whom, on the pier behind his house.

It might be unrelated, but I wonder.

Her sister is the same way. She saw me watching a movie where a woman was eating a human heart.

How can you watch this? she asked, covering her eyes.

I like it, I explained.

I made a movie with my mom.

I made a movie in New Jersey.

We tried to sell a movie about killing each other, which we wrote but never made.

One of our movies had a distributor, but then they changed their mind.

We tried to sell a movie about the time Payton stole a wig that belonged to the Broadway production of Hamilton.

It took me a long time to be able to think of a movie we could make about something that wasn't true.

It took a long time to figure out we could do that.

It took a long time to understand that we could make a vampire movie, that it was allowed.

I haven't watched any movies in a long time.

The Mets are always playing when I get home from work.

When I want to make a movie, what I want is to be responsible for what someone else gets to see.

When I start a new job with a new family where I'll be taking care of a new baby, the mother always asks me what are some things I do with the babies I care for.

I tell her that what I do most of all is narrate.

I narrate our time together.

I speak to the baby about what we are looking at.

I tell the baby what he is seeing.

A movie can be like that, too.

It feels good for a brain to be told what it is seeing, to be directed in its seeing by a generous other.

One reason life is hard is that we have to constantly make meaning where there is none in order to proceed in any direction.

At least, in a movie, a certain fixed amount of content is framed so that we only have to make meaning out of a much smaller, more specific number of ideas, people, events, places.

And we have the knowledge that if we can't, if we don't, or if the meaning we are making by watching is unpleasant, even if we don't decide to get up and turn it off or leave the theater or close the computer, it will end fairly soon no matter what.

When I say we make meaning where there is no meaning, I'm not describing something weak or futile.

I'm describing something beautiful about us, and tragic.

I do some of my best thinking while pushing a stroller up and down Central Park West.

Augie eats his crackers and grapes from his snack cup and I think about a movie.

I think the big secret of making movies is that it's easy, even though it's hard.

That most things are easy.

That the whole world of things, all the hierarchies, all the job titles, the established ways of doing things are tricks to make you feel like you can't do anything.

But anyone can make a movie, because making a movie, like everything else you can do while you're alive, is easy.

I literally never talk to adults.

What I want the boys to learn, what I want to teach them, is that they can do anything.

You can do anything. Because if you just do it, then you're doing it.

I'm afraid I sound like an idiot. That the voice in my brain is the voice of Ricky Bobby.

Augie drops his snack cup on the ground.

I pick it up.

One of the earliest movies I made with Jake and Will and our DP Julian was called the Bipedal Bee.

It was a short musical comedy about a bee who moves to New York City to live out the remainder of his short lifespan and, hopefully, find love.

I knew I'd love the three of them forever when we arrived after dark at the beach at Coney Island, carrying a camera that Julian had checked out of the equipment room at his college, a flashlight, and a cheap bee Halloween costume, which Will put on over a small pair of swim trunks.

It was cold.

The moment I knew was the precise moment when we each stepped from the sidewalk onto the sand, not one of us hesitating to question what exactly it was we were doing with our lives.

When it was time to make the vampire movie, I sent the script to Julian.

He never responded, and because I know him, I knew this meant he did not want to shoot this film, but he didn't want to tell me that.

I felt hurt and confused, but we did not talk about it directly for a long time.

Apparently, he was having an identity crisis somewhere in Queens, which he explained to me later.

In the meantime, we would have to find a new DP.

We took recommendations from friends, we were pointed toward databases, we pored over reels we found on well-made websites and wondered who we could afford.

I stumbled upon the website of a cinematographer named Charlotte.

There was one shot in one sample video I saw that made me feel like they were the one.

It was a tracking shot of a suburban street in low light just after dawn.

The camera moved with whatever light sources Charlotte had placed on the dolly, so that the headlights and taillights of every car parked along the curb on either side of the road reflected subtle flashes of light back into the camera, making the cars look both off and on.

Dead and alive.

I watched that shot several times, sent Jake and Will a link to the website and said look at this shot.

Whoever shot this will understand what we are trying to do.

I want to make a movie with scream queens and finally, a final girl.

I want to make a movie with a sympathetic killer.

I want to make a movie about a child actor who grows up to kill the director who made him famous.

I want to watch this one particular Manson movie but I've never found it.

I don't like movies about women my age trying to find themselves or romantic love.

I don't want to make a movie about aliens.

I don't want to make a movie about outer space.

Sometimes, I want to make a movie about some of my painless thoughts.

A voice wandering around about the bells and days that had been ruined and other days that had been made.

A gentle movie about whatever Dido was lamenting.

A movie narrated by a vain cabaret legend who you never see.

I want to make a movie in Biloxi.

I want my mother playing herself again, like she did for me once in the car as I directed her from the backseat and Julian held the camera on the passenger side.

Beside me the sound guy who we hired locally squeezed in with the boom and headphones.

When we went hours over on the shoot, he complained about missing his daughter.

And I was in the wrong, and I was sorry and paid him extra.

I want to make a movie in Biloxi and I want Parker Posey to play my mother.

Parker Posey went to high school with Kiowa, my mom's friend who comes over to smoke weed and dye her hair.

Parker Posey is from Mississippi, and because of Kiowa we are just one step removed, which deeply soothes me.

One day Milo said he wanted to make a movie about his life.

His dad told him that a movie about someone's life is called a biopic.

I said not many people make the biopic of their own lives.

Yours would be an autobiopic.

He kind of listened to all that, then said that he would play every role.

I'd play myself, my mom, my dad, Augie.

Would you play me? I asked.

I'd play you, he said.

I would love to see that movie, I said.

I would love to see what you do with my character.

I'd be constantly telling me, like Milo me, to be careful, he said.

I thought about this, holding his hand, walking away from the preschool, trying to be careful on the stairs, slippery with wet leaves.

At the bar after a reading during which the bartender ceaselessly slammed bags of ice on the counter, I saw Julian for the first time in what felt like years with his new girlfriend.

She called him her little baby.

He told me he was going to analysis, and group analysis, and that, don't call him crazy, he was watching all of the Marvel movies.

I said that sounds... fun?

He said I think I am so depressed.

I said you seem happy.

He said I am happy to see you.

He told me he'd met a locally famous actress on his way to analysis that day.

I had actually recently seen her in a movie that I loved about a group of girls who are obsessed with Jeffrey Epstein.

My other friend's boyfriend found the rat for the final scene of that movie.

He worked in the art department.

He found a dead rat on the street and placed it in the fridge.

I think that movie is an example of what John Waters said movies were for.

A movie is a safe place to put your obsessions, your perversions, the evil things you want to do and see.

It is a place where you can put them so other people have to deal with them.

And the people want to deal with them.

That's the beautiful part.

Payton and I watched a movie called Office Killer at MoMA.

It's the only movie Cindy Sherman directed.

The movie is about a strange woman at a magazine office who starts murdering her co-workers and bringing their corpses to her house where she stages them in the basement as if they're all hanging out and having drinks.

The bodies rot and she puts fresh drinks in their stiff hands and shows them movies on a grainy TV in the basement that belongs to her mother, who incidentally lives upstairs in that very house, and because she's bedridden, has no idea what's going on underground.

The curator who introduced the film said that Cindy Sherman had a terrible experience making the movie, then quickly left the podium.

In the two seconds before the lights went down, I tried to use my phone to figure out what had happened, why she hated it, but all I managed to type into Google was "Cindy Sherman" before I had to put my phone away.

We loved the movie.

On the train we told each other how much we'd love to make a movie like that with each other.

One thing I love about Payton's work is that it is visual but seldom narrative.

One thing he loves about my work is that it is almost always narrative.

One difficult and exciting thing about writing this way is that it's so easy to lose control and start having too much fun.

I could not find a single thing online about Cindy Sherman's experience working on Office Killer.

We tried guessing.

Maybe someone was really mean to her?

Maybe it was about money?

Two days later, on the beach, we told our friend Kenta that we had seen that movie.

He said that was so funny. Nobody sees that movie. Nobody screens it. I love that movie.

He said that when the huge art gallery he worked for started firing everyone and closing offices, he tried to screen Office Killer at a work event because he thought it would be funny.

Being fired is like being killed in an office, get it?

He got in contact with Cindy Sherman's people, but they told him it was almost impossible to get permission to have the film screened.

They said even Cindy can't get it screened.

Though I'm sure she'd love to have it screened for this, they said, it won't be possible.

Will, Jake and I waited in line for Covid tests the day before the vampire shoot was scheduled to begin.

It was early September.

The next day we shot a half day at Jake's apartment.

Three scenes in the kitchen and one shot of me leaving a bodega swinging a wrench.

Charlotte brought with them a blonde-haired, Russian camera assistant named Olga who was so serious that she never referred to a shot as good or bad, only usable or not usable.

Olga pulled focus from the corner of the room, never talking between takes.

The only time I saw her smile was when our producer returned with an iced coffee.

She was laughing at us, not with us.

She said, incredulous, we were holding for iced coffee?

We explained it was a prop for the shot.

She said oh, okay, good, then returned to her work.

We finished the day on time.

We ordered Thai food for the cast and crew and sat on apple boxes, the same kind Tom Cruise stands on when he acts with a female lead who is taller than him.

Charlotte said they have to eat a lot of meat every day, for some reason.

I ate strands of papaya salad with my fingers and listened as they said this and many other things about growing up in France, about their divorce which mirrored my own, and about Christopher Nolan, who they kept calling "the master."

The second day, we shot in a bar called Happyfun Hideaway where our friend is the bartender.

In between takes, I played with the soda gun behind the bar, filling glasses with different combinations of soda, what as children we called suicides.

Olga didn't show up.

Rozz found someone named Sammy who took a rapid test in the corner, then wolfed down an egg sandwich and introduced himself to everyone.

What I learned about Sammy over the course of that day is that he is obsessed with Elton John.

The second half of that day, we shot in the 15th Street subway station.

Weeks before, we had staked out the location for the use of its security camera monitors, which we could shoot and cut together with camera footage to create strange, eerie angles of the vampire moving around the subway station.

Charlotte, Sammy and I stood under the monitors while Will helped Michelle find her marks way down the platform.

Charlotte started shooting, Sammy carried equipment, and I stood watching the small monitor, making sure we were getting what we needed.

A train pulled into the station.

The conductor stuck his head out the window and yelled, What are you doing?

I knew he would try to stop us, so I ignored him.

Hey, what are you doing? he shouted again.

I knew Charlotte was only just now beginning to get the shot.

I pretended I didn't understand what he said and very slowly started walking toward him.

Do you have a permit? he clearly shouted.

I'm sorry, what? I said, trying to buy enough time to get the five second shot we came here for.

You need a permit!

We do? I asked, feigning innocence.

You have to stop filming.

Why? I asked.

Why are you filming the security cameras? We don't know why you're filming. You could be terrorists!

Oh, we're not terrorists, I said. My heart began pounding in my chest.

I already called the cops, he said. They're coming.

I waved my hand at Charlotte, who pulled the camera down from their shoulder.

The train left the station.

We ran to the end of the platform, grabbed Will and Michelle, and left the station as quickly as we could.

When we emerged, it had started to rain.

We wrapped the camera in our shirts and the one plastic bag we had with us, and ran toward the van we had rented.

By the time we were in the van, rain was pouring.

Is this the hurricane? Sammy asked.

None of us knew what he was talking about.

There's a hurricane, he said, flatly.

When we got back to Will's, everyone started drinking wine while we reviewed our footage.

It was usable.

We ate the sandwiches and small bags of candy that we had laid out on a table for the cast and crew.

We checked Twitter and Instagram and found out that there was indeed a hurricane.

That night, Jake had to abandon the van near the Children's Museum because the streets flooded so badly during the storm.

The hurricane snapped trees all over Brooklyn, filled the streets with trash.

Will's basement level apartment flooded.

During the flood, he had to move all of our film equipment to the higher floor where his roommate lived.

Thousands and thousands of dollars worth of rented equipment that there is no way we could pay for.

This was the end of the second day.

On the third day, we were so far inside the project that the real world had disappeared.

We covered the windows in Will's apartment with Visqueen and it became night inside the apartment all day.

We shot the killing scene, the scene that would be set to the expensive pop song we just had to have.

We had negotiated to use it with Universal, telling them we could pay just one third of what they had asked.

Strangely, they agreed.

I made fake blood in the kitchen, swirling red food coloring, corn syrup and water in glass jars.

Michelle got a drop of fake blood on her orange pants.

Jane, who played the girl who is killed by the vampire, moved gracefully around the living room, dancing to the expensive song.

She crumpled under Michelle's embrace, twitched and then stopped twitching.

We had Charlotte hold the wide shot of the scene for a very long time.

We want it to be so long that the viewer keeps wondering if we meant to cut.

If we are serious about holding for so long on this dead girl.

We ordered sushi and ate it in the back yard.

Everyone was bitten by large mosquitos.

This was the third day, and the next would be our last.

The fourth day was a night.

Michelle ran down the path in Prospect Park in leather pants and heels.

I ran after her in a blue checked dress and oxfords.

Charlotte ran after both of us, carrying the 30-pound camera rig.

We ran the path many times, trying to avoid certain ugly shadows we made at certain points along the path.

Sometimes we ran too fast for Charlotte.

Sometimes we ran too slowly.

We drank Monster Energy drinks.

I felt happy.

I ran the bases of the baseball field while Charlotte changed the batteries.

I was acting and directing at the same time.

I felt like my brain was going to explode.

Jake and Will kept saying again, again, again.

It was 2 in the morning, 3 in the morning, 4.

Though it was September, everyone got so cold we started to shiver.

We ate more candy.

We ordered steak burritos from one of the few places that were open.

We ran into the dark patches of trees and crouched when we had to pee.

It took until this fourth, final day for everyone to start getting angry.

The timing was right on this.

On the last day, people are irritated, tired, mean.

Charlotte kept groaning, cursing under their breath.

The sound girl we had hired broke her boom mic and insinuated that we had broken it.

She refused to keep shooting until I said we can pay to fix it later but now we need to finish making the movie.

Can you please tape it? I asked.

She begrudgingly taped the boom pole back together.

At 5 am we wrapped.

Rozz started drinking champagne from the bottle.

I finished eating my steak burrito as I walked to the van.

I collapsed when I got home.

The next day, I experienced separation anxiety from the rest of the cast and crew.

I had a hard time returning to my real life.

I missed the movie.

It was better there, when everyone was living, working, and feeling the anxieties together, inside the same envelope, the envelope of the movie.

Kind of like the collective panic attack in Midsommar.

When you are making a movie, you are in a hyper-driven state of togetherness.

Now I was alone, and exhausted, and bloated from all the candy and the Monster Energy drink.

Jake, Will and I met up and went to a bar, where I ate a few nachos, then laid my head down and fell asleep at the wooden picnic table where countless people had Sharpied their names.

Later that day, Jake and Will sent the footage to our editor, Erin, one of the greatest people in the world.

She replied with hundreds of smiley faces.

I just did something so insane I need to write about it, and though it is not about a movie, it is about artmaking, so it is not unrelated.

In fact, it's about poetry.

I called my dad to tell him I had won a poetry prize and that I would be receiving some money.

In bringing up poetry, which I hardly ever do with my father, he brought up the fact that I had never given him a copy of my first book which he'd asked for many times.

The general reason I have not given him a copy of my first book, or access to anything I've published, is because I'm scared of what he will think of me.

Nobody in my family has ever oriented their life around artmaking.

The specific reason I have not given him a copy of my first book is that on one page, I suggest that he was an inattentive parent.

But he was no more inattentive than any divorced parent. Or any parent at all, probably.

He was no more inattentive than most human beings are.

On the other hand, he might not understand that poetry is just made of words, and you have to use something from your life to apply the words to, because of what language is, and it's not "about" anything.

He might understand it, but only if I told him that.

I think it's natural for him to see it as being about something.

I know that I'm the unnatural one.

My fear that he would see I had written that, in combination with my fear that he would think I was a fucked-up, weird person who had dedicated her life to doing something stupid, caused me to create and execute, late at night, a two-fold plan.

First, I took an X-acto knife from my boyfriend's office and meticulously removed the 29th page of the book.

Then, I wrote my dad a letter.

I wrote about how I loved him and the reason I had not shared this aspect of myself was that I didn't want to scare him or make him uncomfortable.

I wrote about how I had to do what I did, how I know it's hard to understand.

I wrote about how much he and my sister and my mom mean to me.

How I have somehow managed to not care what most people think of me, but how with them, it's harder.

How sometimes I get emotional thinking about the way they might react to what I do.

In the morning, I read it over and burst out laughing.

I could not send this letter.

The letter read like a serial killer's confession.

Several weeks after we finished shooting, our beloved editor sent us an email telling us she had synched the audio with all of the footage.

A week after that she sent us the stringout.

I have loved the term stringout since I first heard it, from the same beloved editor who had just said it again.

All of the takes of the scenes, strung together and cleared of the non-essential beginning and end of each take.

The sounds of our bodies settling, the last few frantic directions, the adjustment of a last light.

Speed. Sound speeding. Action. A breath before the actors begin.

And after. Cut. The actors' faces turning toward the other hidden faces behind the camera, the source of their direction, the smile, cough, shake of tension from the bodies.

All of it gone.

Jake, Will and I sat side by side on my couch, silently watching, noting which takes were strong, what subtly different meaning was made by each slight variation of the scene.

What meaning was made by which angles we had gotten, ideas about what meaning could be made by their potential arrangement.

I had to ignore the sensation of watching myself act.

Separate myself as the actor from myself as the director.

I tried and failed to believe I was watching someone else.

I couldn't wait for the day I no longer had to do this.

We were overjoyed with the other performances, with every shot, with the story we were trying to tell, here in endlessly repeating fragments shuffling around on a laptop screen.

I imagine the takes like shells on a beach, subtly different but corresponding to certain tones or feelings, and I am there to arrange them into the best possible pattern, to discern which are the right shells, to discard the wrong shells.

Shells that to another eye might look exactly the same.

I have always inexplicably imagined the takes this way, with even the physicality of shells. Hard, smooth, a weight that is satisfying to move around.

I do not tell Jake and Will about the shells.

We watched hours of footage for a story that will in the end take eighteen minutes to tell.

We sent an extensive list to Erin.

Here is the cut we think we'd like to see.

Milo's favorite time of the day is the twenty minutes after he takes a bath and before he has to go to bed because in those twenty minutes, he gets to watch part of a movie.

He lives for those twenty minutes.

Once, he chose to skip a pool party because it meant he would get home too late to have twenty minutes of movie time before bed.

Every day I pick Milo up from school in Morningside Heights, I know he will want to hear a story for the bus ride back to his apartment, so on the train from Brooklyn, I start trying think of a new one for that day.

For a long time, I told stories I made up myself, about characters I had created.

A version of the Candyman, who steals people's candy at Halloween, who is addicted to candy, but whose deepest, darkest secret is that he's actually really nice.

I found myself getting anxious on those train rides, creating stories, wondering if one day the stories would run out, if I couldn't go on like this forever, and then, even worse, what if one day my stories weren't good enough?

I remember in elementary school, when I was learning about the principles of narrative, a teacher said something scary.

There are only two types of stories.

Someone comes.

Or someone leaves.
It occurred to me that I could solve this problem by simply telling Milo the plot of whatever movie I had most recently watched.

The most recent movie I had watched, that day, was Suspiria.

I figured there was a way to tell Milo the movie Suspiria without traumatizing him, even though he's four years old.

I told him there was a girl named Suzie Banion in Ohio who loved nothing more than dancing.

She was a strong and powerful dancer who was drawn to one school of dance, the Markos Dance Academy in Berlin.

She ran away from home to join that company, traveling very far over the ocean, arriving in a strange city in a rainstorm.

She banged her fists on the door of the dancers' dormitory until an old dance teacher appeared to let her in from the cold, driving rain.

I told him, of course, there was something strange about this teacher, about all of the teachers, about this school of dance.

That just before Suzie arrived, there had been a dancer who ran away and begged for help from a doctor, who of course would not believe a word she said.

That the teachers were witches.

That the dances were their spells.

And on and on.

I found the only thing I had to change was that the dancers, in the end, were turned into frogs instead of killed and bloodied.

Milo became so obsessed with this story we had to start acting it out every day.

We made his baby brother play the worst witch, the one who couldn't leave the basement.

He said can I watch this movie?

I said yes, but not now.

When? He asked. I need to watch this movie.

One day you can watch all the movies, I said.

That will be the best day, he said.

Then I told him the Creature from the Black Lagoon.

I told him Cat People, but did not say that the cat person mauled people to death after darkness had fallen, so the story became more abstract, less clear.

There was no real problem, except that she couldn't play with her friends at night.

I told him Dracula, the Francis Ford Coppola one.

I, somehow, told him Devil's Advocate.

I told him a version of Cape Fear.

I told him Bring it On.

I told him Little Shop of Horrors with all the songs.

Then Sweeney Todd, the Demon Barber of Fleet Street, without the songs, which stressed him out.

Because he's obsessed with movies, he was overjoyed and confused to find out that I myself make movies.

I told him I was making a movie about a vampire.

He said you have to tell me the whole movie right now, so I did.

He began making up alternate versions of the movie because he couldn't stand that it ended where it ended.

He rewrote the ending thousands of times over a couple of months so that sometimes I couldn't remember where I had imagined the story going myself.

We remixed all the stories, so that the vampires from my movie became friends with Irina from Cat People and with Suzie Banion, the dancer from Suspiria.

One day, when I got to work, he said I make movies, too.

It's my job.

Do you want to come to my movie theater?

Milo had never been to a movie theater because of the pandemic.

He held up a little Halloween toy shaped like a phone, which made different Halloween sounds when you pressed the buttons.

He said this is my phone.

I show each person, one at a time, my movies, here on my phone.

Go get in line and I'll take your ticket.

I stood "in line" outside his bedroom door.

He walked over, pretending to be flustered.

Oh, hi. Yes, welcome, we're... almost ready.

He paused for a second.

Now we're ready. You can go sit on the bed.

I sat down on his bed and he pushed me down until I was lying on my back. He tucked me in with his blankets.

So this is how it works. I show you my movie on my phone, he explained cheerfully.

He held the Halloween toy two inches from my eyes.

I think it's too close, I said.

No, this is how it is, he said.

Then he began murmuring disjointed words and making strange sounds.

I looked at him, instinctively.

No, look at the movie. It's the movie.

I sat looking at the Halloween toy, my vision blurry from trying to focus on something so close to my face, while Milo made quiet sounds by my ear.

When one movie ended, he asked if I wanted to see another.

Of course I did.

He showed me several movies and every time I accidentally looked at his face, which was intensely focused on what he was doing, he gently told me, no, watch the movie.

I laid there, looking at the Halloween toy, which was feeling more and more like a phone, the imaginary movies seeming more and more real, thinking about this version of showing movies.

How Milo had imagined a movie theater and had assumed it was such an intimate experience.

Later, during quiet time, I went back to his movie theater, at his request.

This time the line was much longer. He had to show several other pretend people his movies.

I waited at the door while he pretended to show other people several films.

He told me, when it was finally my turn, that he was a little frustrated by how popular his movies had become.

There are so many people now. It used to be just me and you.

In time, Erin sent us the assembly we wanted to see.

The fact that it is called an assembly gives me solace.

The word expresses the provisionality which it is important to stay acutely aware of while watching an assembly.

This is an assembly of your film with extremely rough sound, rough, temporary cuts, more like gashes, and in which you have not yet had the chance to imagine how each shot will communicate with each other.

Every performance will be off-time. Every cut will be awkward.

Every time I have watched a first assembly of one of our films, I have experienced hot waves of shame and guilt and terror at having made something that is so incredibly shitty.

The fears that enter my mind while watching an assembly include the fear that I've wasted people's time, that I'm so stupid and such a bad artist that I don't deserve friends or any kind of love, that no one must ever, ever see this hideous piece of shit film or they will know how truly awful I am, and that I am actually insane.

Every time I see an assembly I decide I will never make a movie again.

Jake, Will and I watch.

After a few moments of silence, someone begins.

The movie is in there, we say.

I can barely see it, but it's there.

I cover my eyes with my hands.

I squeeze the flesh of my face and vow to never make another movie again.

We go through the horrific assembly several more times, making notes for Erin as if our lives depend on it, because they do.

Fearing for our souls.

The same week, while I was at work, helping Milo and Augie put on their coats for an evening stroll to the playground, I received three text messages from Charlotte, the DP who had worked on the film.

In these texts, sent as group texts to me, Jake, Will and Rozz, our producer, Charlotte let us know that they had not yet received their payment, that we were trying to fuck them over, that they felt betrayed because they had really liked us, and several other very passionate declarations of how we had failed them as human beings and friends, which we were not.

Friends, that is.

Milo asked me what was wrong.

I said I had gotten some text messages from someone who was very upset with me.

He waited, standing by the door, talking in a low voice to Augie, who was already in the stroller, so that he wouldn't start crying or fussing, while I immediately responded.

I'm sorry you haven't been paid, Charlotte. I know nothing about payment. Our producers were handling that.

And I am sorry you are having such strong negative feelings. We enjoyed working with you and value everything you contributed to the film.

Rozz immediately responded as well.

Your check is with your agent, she said.

Once, I went to a party at a friend's new boyfriend's parents' apartment downtown.

This apartment looked strangely familiar.

Especially the bathroom.

My friend whispered in my ear.

This is Glenn Close's apartment in Fatal Attraction.

And it was!

I will not be the first to say a movie is like a drug.

I know that a movie is a drug because more than once, when Kyle and I have decided to watch a movie at night, the time of night when I invariably, every single night of my life, am consumed with the anxiety that I am a fucked up person, as the 20th Century Fox logo appeared to signify the beginning of a movie, I have been compelled to squeeze in one last expression of my guilt before the drug kicks in.

I'm a bad person, I say one final frantic time before the opening shot.

It's possible that the narcotic nature of movies is a negative force in our lives just because of the relief it gives us from, in my case, what could be productive self-critical thinking or reflection.

What if, without the opportunity to numb the feeling that I am a fucked up person by watching a horror movie, I was forced to actually figure out whether or not I am a fucked up person, and in what way I am fucked up, and then find a solution to that problem, so that I could be more valuable to my world and community.

What if I couldn't watch a movie and because of the lack of something to distract me, I could find the hidden path to boundless love.

What if this is the kernel of truth inside the saying movies don't kill people, people kill people.

As if movies are what allow people to kill people.

Who knows what I'm trying to say.

Kyle and I went to the movies on our first date.

We saw Uncut Gems and he kept trying to talk during the movie, so I kept wincing and turning away.

I thought we would never be able to have a healthy relationship.

He also kept loudly eating dumplings.

Months later, he stands by his decision to tell me something during the movie.

I thought you would want to know I had been to that exact same Mohegan Sun casino.

To see Katy Perry with my ex-girlfriend.

You have to admit that is something you'd want to know about.

And he was right. I thought that was awesome.

I was asked to act in someone else's movie based on my performance in my own, but in my own I was portraying myself.

My mother's daughter, my sister's sister.

But in this one I was asked to play the protagonist's Cousin Lisa, a totally made-up person, an uptight woman who worked a real job in the city.

She hated vegan pizza and made her cousin feel like shit for not knowing what she wanted to do as a job.

As Cousin Lisa I told this girl who was the star of the film, who had a French accent but was meant to be from Florida, that she was going to end up back in Florida or dead.

My scene was cut from the film for redundancy, the director claimed.

Over email, he asked if I'd like him to send me the edited scene, but I declined and wished him luck.

Adam Driver doesn't watch any of the movies he's in.

He freaked out and left Terry Gross's show because she tried to make him watch part of one.

I don't get why she would try to make him do that.

I think that was pretty mean.

For Thanksgiving that year, my mom came to town, so she, Jake, Will and I made spaghetti and meatballs and cherry crumble.

Our friend Jessa came over with homemade arancini.

We ate weed gummies and then smoked so much actual weed that we could barely move from our seats on Will's couch.

Somehow, by some perfect act of God, we realized we wanted to watch Shrek.

My mom said she had never seen Shrek.

I screamed like a woman in a horror movie. How was that possible?

We put it on.

Watching Shrek on this night was one of the most beautiful experiences of my life.

I remember staring at the beautiful faces of my friends as they watched, wide-eyed and mouths open in unselfconscious joy, the Gingerbread Man and Lord Farquad do the muffin man scene we had seen so many times as children.

I realized the donkey from Shrek has the most loving and pure personality.

I sat on the floor in awe of the donkey from Shrek and his attitude toward life itself.

Shrek sadly says everyone is afraid of me when they meet me.

Donkey says Shrek I wasn't afraid of you.

Shrek says I know, Donkey, I know.

I had tears in my eyes.

I had felt what Shrek was feeling.

I put my hand on Jake's leg and said I want to watch Shrek with you in the nursing home when we're old.

I can't wait to do that with you, he said, not looking at me, but staring at the screen.

I had a disposable camera in my purse.

I put the flash on and looked through the viewfinder at the TV.

I waited for a close up of Shrek.

Shrek emerged from between some vines in the woods.

I took a flash photo of the TV screen and yelped.

Everyone has to try this.

It feels like you are really taking a picture of Shrek.

We passed the camera around between us, literally screaming in ecstasy every time someone would take another flash photo of Shrek.

The person who took the photo would scream, It's real.

I'm walking up to Shrek and taking a flash photo of him.

I've never been so happy.

When I got the film developed, of course, all you can see is the flash reflecting off of the TV screen.

Of the six photos we took of Shrek, in only two of them can you vaguely see Shrek's face, and only if you're looking for it.

I gave the photos to Will for his birthday.

My friend Paavo made a thirteen-minute movie about how oyster shells can be used to fight climate change by arranging them in synthetic reefs in the Gulf of Mexico.

My friend Jane made a movie about kidnapping a child she was babysitting to go to the park and do a spell for love.

She made a different movie about kissing a friend on a bad day, and a different movie about implied sexual violence toward a drug dealer and friendship.

My friend Phil made an animated movie about twins who grow up in a horrible world.

My friend Bo made a movie about a legal dispute between his aunt and the rest of his family.

His Aunt Sharon locked his Uncle John out of his grandmother's house after she died, even though while she was alive the grandmother always said they should take care of Uncle John.

The movie is about being gay in Alabama, the genius and the tragedy of Southern women, and a cedar chest that has never been opened.

It is about a radio show called Trade Line where people call in to sell things within their community which was an early form of social media only existent in Gadsden, Alabama.

That movie my friend made won best documentary at Tribeca the year of the pandemic.

I went to the screening of his movie at Hudson Yards, near the structure that closed because people wouldn't stop jumping to their deaths from its upper floors.

It was summer.

A crowd formed at one edge of the outdoor park because someone spotted Paris Hilton who was leaving the previous screening, which was a screening of her own movie.

She made a movie that year about wanting to make a billion dollars and about the abuse she suffered as a teenager at one of those reform institutions in the desert for teenage girls who get in trouble.

I took photos of her before she disappeared into a white van with her fiancé.

For my friend's screening, we sat outside in beach chairs, placed far apart to deter the spreading of the virus, and were given purple trucker hats to wear with the title of the film scrawled across the front.

He is now trying to make a movie about female snake wranglers at Honey Island Swamp.

I want to make a devotional movie.

I want to make a movie out of a Bible story, but Pasolini already made the one I'd like to make.

The Gospel According to Saint Matthew.

God says I will break thee in pieces.

The horse and it's rider.

Ritual and confusion.

Making a movie, you have to decide where all the music goes.

You have to find a place to put all the music.

Between the light which you've broken into shards.

Some famous director said he could take any three pages out of the Bible and make a great movie.

Martin Scorsese tried to warn us about Marvel movies and so many people got mad.

I want to make a movie where the bell at St. Michael rings ten times.

The people coming out cursing twice as much as they pray.

A movie about six Bud Lights and an overactive mind.

A movie about a truck broken down, a blue dress, a pink cloud of wild azaleas in the alleyway.

I want to make a movie about some things I can't forget about.

Making a movie is the best way to send things up and into the light.

My friend Zach went on a first date at Le Crocodile, a fancy restaurant in the Wythe Hotel.

He and his date ordered the whole chicken.

Zach was wearing a suit because he's always wearing a suit on weekdays since he works in finance.

When the chicken arrived, Zach took his first bite and started to choke.

He couldn't breathe and couldn't make a sound but because he was on a first date, instead of panicking, he got up, walked to the bathroom and tried to give himself the Heimlich on the edge of the sink.

It wasn't working and he was beginning to drool and turn red, and yes, to panic.

He walked out of the bathroom but did not return to the table.

He walked calmly to the hotel lobby and saw three men seated on a bench.

He gave them the international sign for choking.

The three men, too, were wearing suits.

The first man asked if it was alright if he touched Zach, if he gave him the Heimlich.

The first man wrapped his arms around Zach, but failed.

The second man did the same, wrapping him in his arms and thrusting his fist upward and into Zach's abdomen.

The second man failed, but Zach found that he could get a little bit of breath, as if a small sliver of space had been cleared in his trachea.

Still, he was choking.

The third man, too, tried and failed.

By now there was a huge crowd around the suited men performing the Heimlich.

The crowd of women in silk dresses and heels holding the arms of their more casually dressed boyfriends grew tighter around Zach on the black and white marble floors which shone under the chandeliers.

Suddenly, Zach coughed up the piece of chicken, just before he was about to die.

He returned to the bathroom, got himself in order, and walked back into the restaurant.

By this time, he had been gone from the table for about fifteen minutes.

His date, Madison, was a bit confused but didn't ask any questions.

Zach did not tell her what happened.

About twenty minutes later, the host of the restaurant approached the table.

Zach and Madison looked up at him expectantly.

He said are you the man who was choking?

Zach glanced at Madison, who was understandably confused, then back to the host and said yes, but I'm fine now.

For legal reasons, the hotel would like for you to be taken to the hospital.

The ambulance is here.

Zach and Madison turned and saw that, parked at the entrance, red lights spinning, was Zach's ambulance.

He paid for the meal, told Madison, who was unsure of what to do, that no, he did not want her to join him in the ambulance, and followed the host outside.

He rode in the ambulance with the remainder of the chicken, which he had had packed up for him before he agreed to leave.

The EMT took his vitals on the way.

At the hospital, it was explained to him that often, when someone chokes, later, a piece of the material may still be there and find itself lodged again in the airway, for instance, while Zach sleeps.

They suggested he have someone stay with him that night.

This had all happened three weeks after his girlfriend of seven years had moved out.

He was just now getting used to living alone.

He left the hospital in an Uber, still carrying the chicken, after a doctor in the emergency room poked around in his mouth and felt his neck.

He got home around midnight.

He sat down at the table in the empty apartment and ate the rest of the chicken.

He asked himself, at that moment, what movie am I in?

I made pasta with peas and squash and cream and ate it quickly.

I walked to BAM at 6:30 to see a movie because I love the main actress who was also in It Follows, a movie I love.

I wanted to see a serial killer movie directed by a woman.

As I walked, I googled the writer.

As I walked, I talked to my mom about how I wasn't sure I wanted to make movies anymore but when I sat down with my Diet Coke alone in the sixth row and the screen lit up, I felt the way I always feel when the screen lights up.

The bright life is what Dante called life outside of the Inferno, the life he left behind.

The bright life.

I always think a movie is the bright life.

And I always want to make a movie.

The woman in the movie is being followed by a strange man through the grocery store.

She escapes by slipping into a movie theater.

The theatre in Bucharest is showing Charade.

She watches while eating popcorn.

I am watching her watch Audrey Hepburn in a movie.

I read an interview with the director of Shiva Baby, Emma Seligman, who said they let women direct comedies, but they never let women direct serial killer movies, direct dark movies, direct the movies of serious men.

Bolaño said he writes because it's amusing, but there are more amusing things.

Being a crime scene investigator, making a movie.

But there is a case you can't solve, the money stops coming, the money you need to make the movie.

So you end up writing either way.

The saddest movie in the world would be a documentary.

The funniest movie in the world would be a documentary too, but the bounds of film, the enclosure of the screen itself makes it so that life is always funnier than a movie.

And the flatness of film, the flatness of the screen, may be what makes it so that life is always sadder than a movie.

Once we had moved through enough preliminary drafts over email and arrived somewhere closer to a rough cut of the movie, we started having editing sessions at Erin's apartment in Cobble Hill.

We hugged in her doorway.

It was snowing.

She looked older than the last time I had seen her, and I realized we must look older to her too.

My dad is staying with me, she said, as we walked into her small railroad style apartment.

An older man with white hair was lying on Erin's carefully made bed, watching videos on his phone.

He sat up to greet us and spoke with the same soft voice that Erin spoke with, something we had always loved about her.

After we passed through the bedroom into the editing studio, she said quietly that he had been watching a lot of conspiracy videos.

We sat down in the room darkened by blackout curtains.

We heard children playing and laughing in the park nearby.

Erin's two cats fought, clawing at each other in one corner.

She sprayed them with a bottle of water and they ran away into a closet.

Let's get started, she said, booting up two computers and two large monitors mounted on the wall.
I love this movie, she said, as the screens brightened.

We returned every couple of weeks, ordering takeout, watching the movie endlessly on the screens.

We made small adjustments, watched the results, adjusted those results, then watched again.

Once, when we were leaving at the end of a session, Erin asked if we would like to see the movie she had been working on.

She had written this one. And it was the first time she had been on set for a production.

I have a completely new understanding of you guys, she said.

I'll send you a link, she said. I'd love your feedback.

The link awaited me when I got home that night.

I pressed play.

I knew from our conversations over the past few months that the cinematographer who often works with the Safdie brothers shot the film.

Erin had been an editor on Good Time, a perfect movie it hurts my heart to think about.

I knew that one of the actors from Dune was in it.

I knew that though Erin was soft spoken and unassuming and I did not feel intimidated by her, she worked with some of my idols in filmmaking.

This is because, apart from being kind and endlessly lovable, Erin is so incredibly good at her job.

When I watched the film, called Power Signal, I felt ill.

It was so beautifully shot and directed and acted.

It was so beautifully edited by Erin.

It was the story of an alien delivery man on an e-bike who had been impregnating women with light babies.

Babies made of light.

I came home from the serial killer movie I saw at BAM and heard my ex-husband's voice in the hallway on the third floor of the building.

An inimitable voice, a voice I married, a tenor who once sang for the Pope, visiting his old cokehead friends, I guess.

In the Sopranos, Christopher Moltisanti wants to make a movie.

He is inspired by John Favreau's Swingers, a movie I also love.

In Swingers, the characters in LA discuss the famous tracking shot from Goodfellas where the camera follows Ray Liotta and Lorraine Bracco's circuitous journey through a nightclub, through the back door and janitor's hallway and storage and the kitchen and finally, through the bar to the best table in the house.

The characters in Swingers talk about how that shot took three days to light, how it's a mark of insanity to dedicate your life to doing something like that.

Of course, later in the film, the Goodfellas shot is meticulously recreated.

In the Sopranos, Christopher, the John Favreau fan, starts writing a movie in Season 1.

The bits of script he writes are so bad, they've found their way onto Sopranos merch from Etsy.

These lines of dialogue full of typos and mixed metaphors break my heart because I know what it's like to want to make a movie without knowing how.

The mob eventually arranges it so that Christopher can make his movie.

The movie he makes reflects the people around him in an unkind light and causes problems for him within the family, which is also his business, until he's ultimately killed.

He doesn't realize you can't make your life into a movie without changing your life.

Once he's dead, the photo the family hangs up in the shop where they conduct their business is a photo of Christopher wearing headphones, sitting in a director's chair, checking the monitor of his own movie.

The image that will last forever is the image of Christopher making a movie.

And the fake movie that he makes within the fake world of the Sopranos, too, will last forever.

A movie can never be unmade, even at that remove from reality.

The people around Christopher could never quite understand why he wanted to make a movie, but I understand why he wanted to make a movie.

Once you make a movie, people start telling you stories from their lives that they think should be in a movie.

My aunt sent me the longest text messages in the world about three different times my grandmother had scared her to death by being crazy, which she was.

She drank bleach to get my grandfather's attention.

She had a third of one of her intestines removed.

My aunt said these stories would all make a good movie, right?

When I didn't answer, she got scared that I thought she was a bad daughter, a liar, a bad person, ungrateful.

This can happen when you want to make something real into a movie, when you see something that has really happened and see that it might be worth showing to someone else in the form of a film.

It feels good, but not only good.

I knew that these were fears she had about herself in relation to her mother which had very little to do with me, but I felt bad, and didn't know how to help.

But I hadn't responded to her texts because I was watching a movie.

I told her I did not think anything bad about her, that mothers can be so scary, that these stories would make a good movie, even though I'm not sure how I would make it.

My own mother now says it all the time, Courtney, you need to turn this into a movie.

Last time she said it, she was sucking on a vape pen in the driver's seat of her Mercedes in a small town off the highway in Alabama.

I was in the back seat.

We were in line for a car wash and at the small podium where you press the buttons to choose which type of car wash you want, she fumbled to open the door because she hadn't pulled up close enough to press the buttons through the window.

She dropped her vape on the ground.

Her friend Christine in the passenger seat started shouting Kiiim, Kiiiim, get it, as my mom almost fell face first out of the car to find the pen.

Once she had, she kept saying Jesus God Damnit, Jesus God Damnit.

Then she chose the option called Ultimate Car Wash, which was the most expensive one, with the most extras, and pressed the button.

The wooly columns in the car wash began to rotate.

She was somewhere in the middle of telling a story to her friend Christine, and I had started filming her on my Sony Handi Cam.

When she realized I was filming her she said you need to make a movie out of this, even though she saw that I already was.

I mean a real movie, she said.

It will be three women in a car going into the car wash.

They're talking really fast, telling all these stories, but when the car comes out of the carwash, the car is empty.

The women are gone.

She held her hand out as a flourish, palm up.

She gazed at her empty palm as if it was the empty car emerging from the car wash.

And you call it, Ultimate Car Wash.

On the street, where I pick up almost anything that interests me and bring it into my home, I found a large blue book called THE MOVIE GUIDE: THE MOST COMPREHENSIVE FILM REFERENCE OF ITS KIND.

I put it on the shelf and forgot about it.

Today, I finally opened it to a random page and found the entry for Beaches, a movie I have never seen.

"In reality BEACHES is a trite, maudlin, and terribly superficial effort of the sub-made-for-tv-quality, an insult to anyone who has ever befriended another human being."

This book is the size of a Yellow Pages and completely filled with reviews just like this one.

I was so shocked I slammed the book closed and burst out laughing.

I had thought, for the months that it was sitting on my shelf, that it was a book that explained as neutrally as possible what every movie was about.

The things it says about some of the movies, I wouldn't say about my worst enemy.

As it always happens, the final cut snuck up on us.

One night, watching with Erin, after making one last adjustment, we saw it.

Here was the movie we had been working for two years to make.

Our movie was one of the strangest short films I'd seen in a long time, and was different than what I expected it to be.

At the same time, we could not deny it was the exact thing we had been trying to make.

I felt like Lady Macbeth looking at the blood on her hands.

Something that had been forming inside me was now made real.

I had seen it in my imagination once, then for a long time, while I was making it, I couldn't see it.

Now suddenly it was back.

But not the way I imagined it, because now it was real.

It showed itself to me. It looked back at me, and was different than I expected.

It knew itself better than I could.

That's the thing. You think you're in control, but one day your movie shows itself to you.

Jake, Will and I stopped at a bar on our way back to Crown Heights.

What a weird movie to have wanted to make, we said.

And we were so happy.

I described Blockbuster video to Milo.

I tried to tell him how amazing it felt to be released with your sister into the Blockbuster, to hear your mom's voice saying, "You can each pick a movie."

My sister's way of watching a movie is different from mine.

She only likes to watch a movie if she's seen it many times before, but I was always confused because there is no movie you could watch for the first time if you needed to have already seen it.

So sometimes, ostensibly, she watched a new movie.

When she found one that would become part of her rotation, it was without ceremony.

John Tucker Must Die, She's The Man, and Heavyweights. These were her movies.

She has never wanted to make a movie.

When I was a child, I put on a movie every night to help me go to sleep, pushing the same one back into the VCR whenever I was too tired to pick a new one.

I fell asleep watching the movie, and woke up to the static a little while later when I had to pee.

I'd then turn the TV off, go to sleep, and start again the next night.

At some point I began to enjoy the repetition and crave it.

I got into the habit of changing the movie only at the end of every nine weeks, which is how our school years were divided.

When I got a progress report, I changed the sleep movie.

But once I changed it, I would not be able to watch that movie ever again.

I couldn't stand it.

The sleep movies I remember most were Harriet the Spy, Matilda, and Inspector Gadget. Nine weeks of each.

The night Michael Peterson maybe killed his wife, maybe killed the second woman he killed in his life, he rented America's Sweethearts.

Christopher Walken is in it.

The serial killer Jeffrey Dahmer made some of the people he killed watch a movie first.

The Exorcist 3.

A cinematographer, a young woman working on her first feature, was killed by the actor Alec Baldwin who shot her with a gun he did not know was loaded.

On the weekends, sometimes, Kyle and I start a movie in the morning and watch it over the course of the day in small increments while we eat our meals.

During the week, we start a movie Monday night, and watch it in similar small increments at dinner time over the next couple of days.

Many people could not watch a movie like this.

Matthew Wong, the painter, before he died, would watch a whole movie every single night.

I don't know how I came to know that, or even if it's true.

A few years ago, a director I'd met at a film party asked me if it would be weird if she hired me to babysit her kid.

I was like, no. That's what I do for money. It would be nice, actually.

A few days later, I arrived at her mother's apartment on the Upper West Side, where I'd be babysitting the little boy.

A classic six, with orchids on the mantle.

This is the perfect apartment, I said to Shaina.

Oh, I know, she said. It's disgusting. It was actually used as Michael Douglas's apartment in Fatal Attraction.

My heart stopped beating.

I looked around me. It really was Michael Douglas's apartment in Fatal Attraction.

Are you okay? she asked.

Yes, it's just that, well, wow, I—

I gathered myself.

I've been in both now. The Glenn Close apartment too.

I wondered if anybody else who wasn't actually working on the film at the time has been in both of these apartments.

No way, she said. You have to be the only one.

When I was on unemployment during the pandemic, I watched two movies a day.

I wrote long emails to Brittany, my old co-teacher from the preschool, about what I did each day.

She wrote the same kind of emails to me.

I told her about the movies.

I asked her if it was okay to watch two movies a day.

She said yes, it was okay.

I wrote to her about The Canterbury Tales and the Decameron by Pasolini.

I wrote to her about Black Narcissus.

During that time, I felt closer to an understanding of what it meant to make a movie.

I was moved by almost every one I watched.

Moved by the act itself.

I thought about how people wanted to tell stories so badly that over time, more and more expensive and complex technology that required huge crews of people to operate it had been invented for the purpose of telling a story in the form of a movie.

We had to make the images move.

People have died trying to make the images move.

And people have died just trying to see the images move.

I watched a movie about a huge store of nitrate film found buried in a swimming pool in Alaska.

The movie told, in clips from this cache of beautifully preserved film from the beginning of moving images, the story of film itself.

The concept of screaming fire in a theater is something carried to us from the time of nitrate film, when a movie was a cumbersome set of reels of extremely volatile, flammable silver nitrate.

Theaters caught fire constantly and spontaneously.

These cumbersome, volatile movies slowly toured the country by train, reaching the far North very last.

A movie might reach the Kodiak three years after it premiered in New York City.

The people in Alaska were starved for the new moving image, waiting there at the end of the line.

And once a movie had gotten to the end of the Northern line, none of the distributors or studios wanted them back.

Because a movie, then, was a storage and safety liability.

Many films ended up discarded in an empty community pool in a basement of a building in a small city in Alaska.

The pool was covered, with the film inside, by a roller-skating rink, then an ice-skating rink, then it was simply a closed-off, rarely visited basement in a municipal building.

In the 2000s, when the building was finally being torn down because of disuse, the excavators found all of these pristine nitrate films, films of which no copy had survived anywhere else because they had burst into flames in warehouses, theaters, everywhere.

But these movies had been kept stable and cold in this underground, abandoned swimming pool for nearly a hundred years.

The movie I watched about the movie reels found in the empty swimming pool was scored by the band Sigur Ros.

It was all told in titles on the screen, just as the stories are told in the early silent movies the movie was about.

This beautiful movie was also about the history of the Kodiak gold rush.

This weekend, I wanted to see a movie, so I looked to see what was playing.

A new Cronenberg movie had just come out, so I decided to see it later that evening.

Kyle asked what David Cronenberg had directed, trying to put a style of movie with the name.

I said Scanners, Videodrome, Dead Ringers, and I couldn't think of any more off the top of my head, so I googled a list of all of his movies ranked.

Kyle hadn't seen any of them, and I was jealous.

But on the list was a film called Dead Zone, a movie based on a Steven King novel that Kyle was just finishing that very morning.

In fact, over coffee just moments before, he had told me the premise of the novel.

What a coincidence.

We found Dead Zone streaming for free on a friend's HBO Max account and started watching.

Kyle got bored of it because, well, he had just read the novel.

He only had a few pages left.

He went for a walk while I finished the movie.

When I worked in a vegan cheese shop, my favorite coworker Christina would help us pass the long, boring shifts making cashew cheese by telling me the plot of a new Stephen King novel each day.

She had read them all several times.

Her favorite, which she never told me, because she was saving it for last and I got a new job before she got to it, was called Tommyknockers.

All she would tell me was that it was impossible to make into a movie.

And that it had to do with a small town in Maine where someone found part of a UFO in their yard, so the people from the town began to excavate it, but the more of the vessel they exhumed, the more the people in the town started changing.

They began building things without knowing why, they began creating new technologies.

They found a body of some kind of life form in the ship once they had dug out enough, and by then the people were enacting a completely other civilization altogether.

They were, unbeknownst to themselves, repairing the ship, using tools they had built and methods they had learned seemingly from nowhere, as if the ship emitted a vapor of some kind that changed them into another kind of life form.

Meanwhile they were still, like, alcoholics in Maine.

I guess Christina did tell me a lot.

I assume it's impossible to make into a movie because there is no bad guy.

Maybe it's impossible because it does not follow either one of the two plots.

Someone arrives or someone goes away.

I guess the dead alien body arrives.

Years later in a sailor-themed bar near K-town in Los Angeles, a TV writer I had met three days before told me he was speed reading a Stephen King novel that he had been assigned by some studio.

They wanted to adapt it into a movie.

I asked which one.

Tommyknockers, he said.

I screamed. I was drunk.

You've read it? he asked.

No, I said, then told him about the cheesemaker Christina, about how Tommyknockers is the one you can't make into a movie.

He laughed and said he thought he'd found a way.

Later that night he said the secret is you have to say yes to everything.

Everything? I asked. Everything, he said.

For example, in a few minutes, a young man is going to walk through that door who cold emailed me because he liked a TV show I used to write for.

He asked if he could pick my brain.

Most people say no, but I always say yes, to everything, and it's going be weird, he said, and that's what I like about it.

And just before he left to talk to the strange young man who did indeed enter the bar after a few minutes had passed, right when the writer said he would, the writer said, you know, your co-worker, the one who tells a new Stephen King novel every day, she'd make a great character in a movie.

We worked with a composer in LA who found us online.

While we spoke to him on Zoom, a rooster crowed in his yard.

Over the next few weeks, he made a score for our vampire movie that used organs, riffed on Bach.

We gave him as much money as we could afford to.

We worked with a sound editor, someone we knew socially and wanted to work with.

He took a long time and fucked up our movie so badly that we were traumatized by watching it.

We paid him some amount of money, reeling in disbelief at how bad of a job he had done, then went on to hire someone else who did the edit quickly and efficiently and perfectly.

And one day, our movie was done.

There was nothing else we could do to it that would not somehow be undoing it.

Once it was done, I stepped away. I started writing something else.

Jake and Will took on the responsibility of figuring out what we would do with the movie.

We sent it to festivals.

We are now awaiting rejection or acceptance.

I have to watch a movie for my acting class, which I am taking in order to become a better director of my own movies.

My teacher chose the Wizard of Oz.

In the Turner Classic Movies intro, a blonde woman at the Met explains the film is being presented in a series about fashion in film.

The Wizard of Oz, of course, features some of the most iconic costuming in film history.

The first Tin Man, an actor who later became famous in the Beverly Hillbillies, was hospitalized because he inhaled too much of the aluminum dust that was used to make his hands silver.

For the next Tin Man they hired, aluminum paste was used instead.

Due to his facial prosthetics, the Cowardly Lion had to take his meals through a straw.

And a 76-year-old man recently pleaded guilty to smashing a glass case in the Judy Garland Museum in Minnesota to steal the Ruby Slippers.

He had never seen the movie and simply believed the shoes had real rubies on them.

When he peeled them off and tried to sell them, he was informed they were made of glass.

How many times must I have seen the Wizard of Oz to know every word of every song?

The Tin Man sings If I Only Had a Heart.

"Just to register emotion / jealousy, devotion."

When they met the Cowardly Lion, I was crestfallen.

I will never make anything as good as this.

Life's been simply unbearable, he says.

It's been in me so long I just have to tell you how I feel.

To watch the Wizard of Oz at 7 am is a religious experience.

Poppies, poppies.

I began sobbing when Dorothy tried to tell the Tin Man, the Lion, and the Scarecrow how hard it was for her to say goodbye.

While the tears were still on my cheeks, Kyle came out of the bedroom, eyes puffy from sleep, and asked,

how do you feel about a movie?

It took me a moment to realize he was talking about a tentative plan we had made to go to MoMA that afternoon to see Let's Scare Jessica To Death.

I wiped my face and said I feel good about it.

Acknowledgements

Thank you Jake Goicoechea and Will Carington for the bright life.

Thank you Jessa Ross, Jamie Fitzpatrick, Brittany Miller and Anne-Louise Brittain for reading versions of this poem.

Thank you Kim and John Bush for showing me your favorite movies.

Thank you Rozz Therrien, Charlotte Dupre, Michelle Uranowitz, Jane Stiles, Julian Kapadia, Richard Perez, Payton Barronian, Sam Duarte, Bo McGuire, Andy Weber, Laura Henriksen, Ben Fama, Ari Lisner, Dan Arnés, Kentucker Audley, Tynan De Long, Milo Bellow Chalfin, Augie Bellow Chalfin, my little sister Gabe Snodgrass and everyone else I've had the unbelievable fortune to make and watch and talk about movies with.

Thank you Bill Lavender and Sean F. Munro for your energy, time, and work in making this poem into a book, which is the best thing in the world, except for a movie.

Rejoice In The Lamb, the 18 minute vampire movie in development in this poem, played at Santa Barbara International Film Festival, Sun Valley Film Festival, Tacoma Film Festival, InsideOut Toronto, Brooklyn Horror Film Festival, and Montclair Film Festival. It can be viewed at NoBudge.com and on Vimeo.

About the Author

COURTNEY BUSH is a poet and filmmaker from the Mississippi Gulf Coast.

Lavender Ink
New Orleans
lavenderink.org

www.ingramcontent.com/pod-product-compliance
Lightning Source LLC
Chambersburg PA
CBHW020333170426
43200CB00006B/364